GW00320446

PLANTS FOR THE

HERB
GARDEN

PETER THURMAN

First published in Great Britain in 1994 by
PAVILION BOOKS LIMITED
26 Upper Ground, London SE1 9PD

Conceived, edited and designed by Russell Ash & Bernard Higton
Picture research by Julia Pashley
Plant consultant Tony Lord

A CIP catalogue record for this book is available from the
British Library.

ISBN 1 85793 109 2

Printed and bound in Singapore by Tien Wah Press

2 4 6 8 10 9 7 5 3 1

This book may be ordered by post direct from the publisher.
Please contact the Marketing Department.
But try your bookshop first.

CONTENTS

INTRODUCTION

WHAT IS A HERB?

To botanists the term 'herb' is short for herbaceous plant — that is any non-woody plant that invariably dies back to ground level every winter. It can be an annual, biennial or perennial.

To gardeners past and present however, the word encompasses any plant, woody or herbaceous, that has leaves, stems, flowers or even roots that are used, fresh or dried for a wide variety of purposes.

Historically, the most important use of herbs has been for medicinal purposes, closely followed by their culinary use — for flavouring and embellishing food (as well as preserving it) and for making teas. Seeds used in cooking are usually called spices. Herbs are also used to make perfume and other products in the cosmetics industry, and many dyes are derived from herbs.

HERBS PAST AND PRESENT

There is something deeply satisfying about growing herbs or creating a herb garden, due, no doubt, to the fact that their cultivation and use is intricately entwined with our history and evolution. Throughout the ages, representations of herbs have appeared on the artefacts of many cultures —

A SMALL HERB GARDEN OF SAGE, MINT, LEMON BALM AND OTHERS.

HERBS FORMED THE BASIS OF MOST EARLY MEDICINES.

from Egyptian tomb paintings, Babylonian cuneiform tablets, Chinese bronzes, Greek vases, stone slabs and columns of the Mayans, Pompeiian frescoes, Khmer bas-reliefs, Persian and Mughal paintings to European monastic manuscripts dating back to medieval times, demonstrating their widespread use and important place in cultural history.

We may speculate that somewhere, sometime, someone must have taken the plunge and eaten a particular leaf for the first time. Perhaps they were attracted by the smell, since many herbs have aromatic leaves or flowers. It must have been trial and error, probably involving fatalities, but if a plant seemed to help cure a malady or enhance the taste of food, the knowledge was passed on from one generation to the next.

Herbal medicine has been practised all over the world for thousands of years. Plants were the main source of therapeutic products to treat injury and disease. Examination of pollen grains found in a 60,000 year old Neanderthal grave in Iraq identified seven species of plants that are still in use in that area today as medicines. Other archaeological studies have revealed that herbs were used to preserve food 50,000 years ago. It is known that around 2000 BC, the Babylonians used caraway, coriander and other herbs as medicinal cures.

The ancient Egyptians imported many herbs, spices and aromatic oils from India and Babylon. Thyme, garlic, saffron, fenugreek and many others were put to good use – in cooking, as medicines, dyes, antidotes to poisons and even in worship and, of course, for embalming purposes.

Our accumulated knowledge of herbs and herbal uses was documented in the form of lists in what are known as Herbals. In 2800 BC the Chinese herbalist Shen Nung noted over 300 plant drugs. The Greek physician Hippocrates studied herbs in the fourth century BC and produced a comprehensive record of contemporary herbal usage. In the first century BC Dioscorides wrote about the medicinal uses of over 500 plants and herbs in what is considered to be

A MEDICINAL PLANT DEPICTED IN A 13TH-CENTURY MANUSCRIPT.

the prototype for herbals, *De Materia Medica*. This was followed by many others, one of the most famous being the English author Nicholas Culpeper's *The English Physitian* [sic] (1653) later known as *The Herbal,* which appeared in numerous editions during suceeding generations.

In western Europe, during the Roman occupation in the early centuries AD, the ancient knowledge of herbal values and the cultivation of herbs for culinary and medicinal purposes greatly increased. In Britain the Romans introduced over 200 varieties of herbs, including many of today's favourites such as fennel, borage, sage, parsley, rosemary and thyme. Others, such as comfrey and yarrow, have in fact naturalized in our gardens, waste places and hedgerows.

In medieval times, with the establishment of the Christian Church, monks, who cared for the sick established physic gardens in the grounds of their monasteries. These early herb gardens provided the raw materials for medicine and monks became more skilled in horticulture than any other section of the community. Their knowledge and skill was much in demand. Herbs were used not only to cure ills but their role in preserving and improving the flavours and smells of food was very important to the ever-increasing, ever-poorer European population. The monastic physic garden was usually cultivated by the monk in charge of the infirmary. The herbs were grown, occasionally with vegetables, in individual, narrow and rectangular beds for ease of picking and in order to prevent unfortunate mistakes in administering the wrong remedy.

For two thousand years other exotic herbs and spices had been brought to Europe from India by sea to the Persian Gulf, and then by land to the Mediterranean, and from the Far East by the Silk Road which led from Peking to Constantinople. It was the loss of these sources that prompted drastic action by Elizabethan seaman adventurers in seeking out new sources of supply. The lure of scents and spices in medieval Europe was almost stronger than that of fine fabrics and gold. The importance of smell and taste, and the craving to satisfy those senses, is hard to understand fully today. Try to imagine the pervading stink of even the finest of medieval homes and the dullness of medieval food – the unvarying diet of bread and meat – often decaying, with dried fish in Lent and on Fridays. By the end of the Middle Ages the tastes of the rich had outstripped what was available in Europe; they longed for anything that would

A PAGE FROM AN EDITION OF JOHN GERARD'S *Herball*.

1 *Verbascum Matthioli.*
French Sage.

‡ 2 *Verbascum angustis Salviæ folijs.*
The lesser French Sage.

‡ 3 *Phlomos Lychnites Syriaca.*
Syrian Sage-leaued Mullein.

¶ *The Description.*

1 WIld Mullein, wooddy Mullein, *Matthiolus* his Mullein, or French Sage groweth vp like a small wooddie shrub, hauing many wooddy branches of a woollie and hoarie colour, soft and downy: whereupon are placed thicke hoarie leaues, of a strong pontick sauour, in shape like the leaues of Sage, whereupon the vulgar people call it French Sage : toward the top of the branches are placed roundles or crownets of yellow gaping floures like those of dead Nettle, but much greater. The root is thicke, tough, and of a wooddy substance, as is all the rest of the plant.

† 2 There is another sort hereof that is very like the other, sauing that the leaues & euery other part of this plant, hath a most sweet and pleasant smell, and the other more strong and offensiue: the leaues also are much lesser and narrower, somwhat resembling those of the lesser Sage.

‡ 3 I thinke it not amisse here to insert this no lesse rare than beautifull plant, which differs from the last described in the maner of growing & shape of the floures, which resemble those of the *Lychnis Chalcedonica*, or None-such, but are of a yellow colour. The leaues are hairy, narrow, and sharp pointed; the stalkes square, and root wooddy. *Lobel*

(to

enliven their diet or improve the conditions in their homes and they were willing and able to pay whatever it cost. Grand expeditions were planned and made, and thousands of men risked their lives to bring such spices as cinnamon, cloves and pepper from far off countries, even searching for new places and routes by which to obtain them beyond the limits of the known world. Although the trade continued for a long time, the great expense of importing herbs and spices prompted great efforts to grow the necessary plants at home.

From the 16th century onwards the use of herbs was considered a culinary art. Many market gardens near the larger conurbations specialized in the cultivation of herbs sold in markets or by street vendors. In Elizabethan times, most manor houses had some form of herb garden, quite formal and patterned – the so-called 'knot' gardens of that period – and often included decorative plants such as honeysuckle and roses grown for their scent. Herbs were used not only for curing ills, healing wounds and in cooking, but also for 'strewing' on floors to scent a room – or, more accurately, to mask evil odours.

The enthusiasm for herbs continued into Queen Victoria's reign, but as a result of the popularity of the landscape style of gardening and finally the coming of the industrial revolution and the large-scale exodus of people from rural areas to the towns and cities, the domestic cultivation of herbs was greatly reduced. In urban areas the increasing popularity of just the basic table condiments, patent medicines and 'cure-all' elixirs caused a severe decline in the use of herbs in cooking and as simple remedies. At one point, during the Victorian era, parsley, sage and mint were the only herbs generally used in cooking. By the mid-19th century there was a danger that the knowledge of herbs built up over thousands of years would disappear. Fortunately, in rural cottage gardens and in the less heavily industrialized

KEW'S MODERN REPLICA OF A 17TH-CENTURY HERB GARDEN.

Mediterranean countries, the use of herbs continued without interruption.

Towards the end of the last century two garden writers and designers, William Robinson and Gertrude Jekyll, encouraged the move away from Victorian formalism and extolled the virtues of wild and less formal styles of gardening. Both were influenced by the planting in cottage gardens where fruit, vegetables, herbs and flowers would all share the same bed. They mentioned herbs in the same breath as herbaceous perennials and ornamental shrubs and recommended their use for purely decorative purposes.

Eleanour Sinclair Rohde also wrote many books and articles in the 1920s and '30s drawing attention to herbs. Her own garden was unusual for its time, being based mainly on uncommon herbs and vegetables. She designed many herb gardens for others and we have her to thank more than anyone else for the revival of interest in herbs and herb gardening.

Vita Sackville-West and her husband Harold Nicolson continued this 'arts and crafts' style of gardening into the middle part of this century. Their garden at Sissinghurst is still an inspiration to many gardeners. The formal layout, softened by informal planting in a series of outdoor 'rooms', is still fashionable today and ideal for displaying herbs to their best effect.

On the other side of the coin, during the first half of this century, our vast and ancient understanding of the importance of herbs as medicinal plants was swept aside in favour of mass-produced drugs. It is salutary to remember, however, that many of these 'wonder drugs' were created using plant extracts.

THE USE OF HERBS TODAY

It is only in recent years that people have begun fully to appreciate the value and potential of herbs again. Now we have turned full circle, interest in the herbal cures of old has been revived and the importance of herbs in cooking has been rediscovered and enlarged. Cookery has become a popular pastime and improved communications, travel and world-wide movement of peoples has created a cosmopolitan culture. In Britain, Chinese, Greek, Indian, French and Italian dishes have been joined by Thai, Spanish, Mexican, Vietnamese and Indonesian cuisines – all of them using their own combinations of herbs and spices. Aromatic herbs are even used to enhance the otherwise bland and monotonous taste of fast food. Culinary herbs are now grown on a large scale for sale, fresh or dried, through supermarkets and grocery shops. It is estimated that over 1,400 tonnes of herbs are produced each year in Britain on land occupying over 500 hectares. Such production is commercially signifi-

A STANDARD BAY SURROUNDED BY HERBS, FLOWERS AND VEGETABLES.

cant: a single tonne of freeze-dried chives imported from Denmark costs more than £40,000.

Herbs are again being used to preserve food. Marjoram and rosemary have long been known to curb rancidity in high fat foods, while others are extremely effective in preventing the growth of bacteria and fungi that can infect food.

Fortunately, despite its decline in the late 19th and early 20th centuries, the use of herbs for medicinal purposes never completely disappeared. Today, interest has reached a new peak. The medical profession, previously accused of over-prescribing all manner of modern drugs, is now taking a much more serious and closer look at the potential of herbs. Some modern drugs produce serious side-effects and there is a widespread belief that they have become too complicated and too remote from the 'root' of the problem – they often treat the symptom rather than the cause of the illness. There is a lack of confidence in some drugs that are the result of modern technology and consequently 'natural' remedies are attracting more support.

There are about 250,000 flowering plant species on the planet, 25,000 of which are known to have been used for medicinal purposes. To date, only about 2,500 plants have been thoroughly tested to try to find out how they work. It has been proved that many do contain beneficial substances. Homoeopathy, for example, has become much more widely respected and accepted, even by mainstream medical practitioners. Herbs are also the main source of soothing lotions used by aromatherapists.

'Old wives' tales' and folklore remedies are being closely examined and re-assessed with often remarkable results. Plants that have long been prescribed for specific ailments are proving to contain definite, identifiable compounds such as alkaloids, glycosides, oils, gums, and steroids to which cures can be directly attributed. Many of these substances can be isolated, purified and even synthesized or simulated. For example, for many hundreds of years comfrey has been valued for its ability to help broken bones set and to heal wounds, cuts, swellings, sprains and bruises. Recent research has shown that the plant contains allantoin and choline which promote red corpuscle production that helps a patient recover after excessive loss of blood.

Digitalis has long been prescribed for heart problems. It is now known that this is a valid and effective use due to glycosides contained within the plant that increase the tone of the cardiac muscle, causing the heart to function more 'cleanly'. However, as with many medicinal herbs, the wrong dosage or application can do more harm than good so it is always essential to seek professional advice.

It is becoming clear that plants that have been developing ways of protecting themselves against diseases and viruses for millions of years contain hundreds, perhaps even thousands of chemicals that can be used as medicines. Much of the research into curing cancer and the AIDS virus involves plants and plant extracts, and it is hoped that over the next few years scientists will make further usee of these natural resources in achieving yet more breakthroughs in the quest to cure serious illnesses.

HERBS IN TODAY'S GARDENS

The many and extremely varied uses of herbs, especially as medicines, is a large subject and beyond the scope of this book. Recipes and dosage levels to treat illnesses need to be carefully adhered to otherwise there can be serious adverse effects. Herbal prescriptions are best left to the experts and 'do-it-yourself' diagnoses should be avoided at all costs.

Today, most gardeners use herbs to create gardens, borders or beds that are both beautiful to look at and useful for culinary purposes – nothing beats cutting your own fresh herbs

THE HERB GARDEN, A WATERCOLOUR BY COLIN NEWMAN

for cooking – and the rest of this book concentrates on these two aspects of herb gardening.

Many gardeners have a deep love of herbs. To some they help bring to life the nostalgic and romantic idea of the Victorian cottage garden when rural life appeared to be uncomplicated and slow in pace, in contrast to modern times. Like songs, certain smells can conjur up vivid memories of bygone days. The essential oils that emanate from the leaves of aromatic herbs on a warm summer day or when crushed or prepared in the kitchen may remind you of the garden of your childhood, or be linked to a particular holiday, grandparents or family meal time: mint is forever evocative of roast lamb Sunday lunches.

Although herbs flower and some are very beautiful and scented, the main attraction is their foliage. The range of colour, shape and texture of herb leaves can be mouthwatering. There are silver, grey, gold, purple and variegated types as well as good plain greens and they may be smooth, glaucous or hairy, broad, filigree or minute. Any garden or border designed around foliage rather than flowers will tend to look attractive for a longer period. Many herbs have attractive outlines or overall shapes – rounded domes or creeping clumps. Always try to associate herbs (and other plants for that matter) together in combinations of contrasting textures and harmonised colours. Filigree foliage, such as fennel, looks good when planted next to the broad leaves of comfrey and the upright narrow leaves of chives. Purple fennel associates well with purple sage or perhaps golden lemon balm.

Another significant factor in the popularity of herbs is their size and growth habit. Most of the common species are small and compact and require very little maintenance – perhaps just a clipping over after flowering and cutting back at the end of summer or in early spring. These attributes suit the average garden of today which is small and the lifestyles of many gardeners which can leave little time for gardening chores. Gardens are to be enjoyed but few of us have the time to over-indulge ourselves.

SPECIFIC USES OF HERBS

In containers

Many herbs are happy to be grown in some form of container. This means that you can grow them on a balcony, patio or even in a window box. Container gardening gives maximum flexibility. You can re-arrange displays seasonally so that straggly plants that have been cut back are hidden behind others that are looking their best. Groups of containers can be moved around the garden to wherever is most convenient and best for growth – nearer the kitchen when it is wet, nearer the outdoor tap when there is a drought. Some herbs such as mint have invasive roots, but

PURPLE SAGE WITH PELARGONIUMS IN A GRAND TERRACOTTA TROUGH.

planted in containers they can be kept under control. In borders rampant herbs can be contained by planting them into cheap plastic pots and then plunging them into the ground.

Many herbs prefer a well-drained soil. Those native of Mediterranean regions have evolved to cope with poor soils and long, hot, dry summers. So, if your garden is on heavy clay, growing herbs in containers by-passes the problem. The ability to tolerate dry conditions also means that forgetting to water regularly may not be fatal.

Growing your favourite culinary herbs in a window box outside your kitchen is the ultimate in convenience. Choose the smaller types such as thyme and parsley or the species that are best grown from seed every year such as basil, otherwise the box will soon look overgrown and scruffy. If you must grow mint in such a restricted place, plant it into a window box inside its own container. For short periods of time you can even grow herbs in small pots on your kitchen window sill. Chives and parsley for example can be regularly cropped for two to three months before getting weak or drawn and needing to be potted-on or planted out in the garden.

Other herbs such as marjoram and tarragon can be potted up in autumn and brought indoors for a supply of fresh leaves through the winter. Similarly, mint can be brought into a warm kitchen in late winter to give an early crop of leaves before growth has started outdoors.

In larger containers, you may wish to try some of the shrubby herbs. Rosemary, bay (perhaps clipped into a pyramid or standard) and sage will all do well. They may be too heavy to move around on a regular basis – unless you put them on castors.

Some herbs, such as the beautiful lemon-scented verbena, are slightly tender. Growing them in containers is ideal – they can be outside in summer enjoying the warm sun and then tucked away into the porch or greenhouse before the first frosts.

Herbs in mixed borders

Many herbs are ornamental enough to be grown in flower borders and beds along with other plants. The larger herbs such as angelica, fennel and lovage will more than cope with being planted next to bulky shrubs and clumps of perennials. In fact they can make a refreshing change. The smaller herbs such as chives, marjoram and hyssop make excellent edging or front of border plants.

Herbs can also be used to fill up the gaps in a newly planted border or where a plant has suddenly died. Herbs that have previously been grown in containers that have become pot-bound can be excellent for this purpose.

With many herbs, you are only likely to need a few leaves in the kitchen at any one time so you will not spoil their decorative effect after cropping. Other herbs such as rosemary and lavender are decorative shrubs in their own right. Bergamot is commonly grown as a flowering plant along with other perennials.

Other uses
Sage makes an excellent weed-smothering ground cover plant. On a smaller scale, thyme and lemon balm are equally effective.

Because of their stature, habit and tolerance of dryness, smaller herbs such as thyme and winter savory make useful rock garden plants – the creeping thymes will also grow between paving slabs and do not mind being walked upon.

Most herbs prefer a sunny, well-drained situation but a few such as sweet Cicely, chervil and borage will grow in a degree of shade. Angelica, comfrey, sorrel and others will cope with heavy clay soils. Remember also that many herbs attract bees and butterflies, which add another dimension to your garden.

MAKING A HERB GARDEN

If you have room you may want to consider turning over part of your garden exclusively to herbs. Although herbs will be dominant, it should not be entirely to the exclusion of other plants such as roses or honeysuckle that combine well with them.

A formal herb garden, perhaps enclosed by a hedge or wall to hold in the aromas, should have a strong, geometric pattern created by gravel or brick paths. The symmetrically arranged square or round beds, perhaps in a cartwheel

AN ENCLOSED AND STRONGLY STRUCTURED HERB GARDEN.

design, edged with clipped box, lavender or lavender cotton can be planted up with a mixture of attractive and useful herbs. Do not be afraid to repeat useful herbs in opposite beds to give a sense of unity.

There should always be a place to sit to enjoy the many scents that will hang in the air and the insects that will doubtless visit the flowers.

A central urn, statue or sun-dial will complete the picture. A simple herb garden can be created in an existing paved area of any size. Just take out a percentage of the slabs, perhaps in a checkerboard pattern and plant up each slab space with a different herb.

Basic herb care guide
Regular cropping of herbs in the growing season encourages good fresh re-growth. In the ornamental herb garden, some herbs will not be under this pruning regime. These may get straggly and spoil the appearance. Such plants should be cut

back quite hard. Some herbs such as fennel, sage and oregano lose their flavour if allowed to flower and set seed, so it is best to remove the flower buds if you want to continue harvesting.

Remember that some herbs are annuals or biennials so they will need to be re-sown. Self-seeding herbs such as borage, fennel and sorrel can either be a joy or a pain depending on how tidy your mind is! If you like a neat, well ordered herb garden, avoid these self-seeders. Non-woody, perennial clump-forming herbs such as bergamot and mint should be lifted every three to four years.

Using herbs in the kitchen

Cutting herbs from your garden as and when needed and using them in cooking, salads and teas is in most cases ideal. However, some herbs are even better dried and their flavours will be retained for many months. The best time to gather leaves for drying is early morning before the sun gets too high in the sky. Try not to damage or bruise the leaves, and shake off any raindrops or dew. Wash the leaves only if they are dirty. Diseased or pest-ridden leaves should, of course, be rejected. Correct drying is a gradual, steady process. The temperature should be 21–33°C (70–90°F) in a well-ventilated but dry place – an airing cupboard with the door left slightly ajar is an ideal location. Lay the leaves on trays on tissue in a single layer or hang in bunches. The leaves will probably change colour and become brittle but should not turn to powder when rubbed. Store the dried leaves in air-tight containers in a dark cupboard. Roots are best dried in the sun. Herbs should not be handled during or after the drying process and dried material should not be mixed with fresh. For freezing, place the leaves into small polythene bags without blanching. Alternatively fill the compartments of an ice cube tray with chopped herbs and top up with water.

PLANTS DIRECTORY

This is far from an exhaustive list of herbs,
particularly of those used for medicinal purposes.
Great care should be taken when using herbs
to cure any form of illness, and always
seek professional advice. This list, therefore,
concentrates on culinary herbs which are also
attractive and so have a place in a purely
ornamental garden.

Plants are listed in alphabetical order of common name
followed by the Latin name.

The 'fact line' shows, in order:
Size – average height in metres and spread in metres of a
mature plant
Soil – tolerances, preferences or special requirements
Site – tolerances, preferences or special requirements

Angelica

ALECOST *TANACETUM BALSAMITA* (syn. *BALSAMITA MAJOR*)

A perennial, aromatic herb with greyish leaves and yellow, button-like flowers in late summer. The minty-scented leaves are used in pot pourris or chopped into salads, cakes and soups. They will also flavour roast meat and home brewed beer.

0.9 × 0.8   Any soil   Dry, sunny position

ANGELICA *ANGELICA ARCHANGELICA*

A tall, bold-leaved perennial herb with sweet-scented stems and leaves. The large umbels of small creamy flowers appear in July. This is a most decorative herb, suitable for the back of a border. Angelica has long been used in the confectionery industry. The young stalks are candied and used to decorate cakes and sweets. Liqueurs, such as Chartreuse, and jams are flavoured with Angelica and a little of the root or stem added to rhubarb will reduce the tartness.

2.0 × 0.5   Good, moist soil preferred   Partial shade

Sweet Basil   Bay

BASIL, SWEET *OCIMUM BASILICUM*
This is a low-growing, aromatic annual that is frost tender. It
is usually grown from seed sown every April or May. Basil is a
very popular culinary herb. The fresh leaves are added to
salads or used to flavour soups, stews or any dishes that
include tomatoes, mushrooms, poultry or eggs. On the
Continent basil is also a significant ingredient of *pesto* and
soupe au pistou.

O. b. var. *citriodorum*, lemon basil – more compact with lemon-
scented leaves.

O. b. var. *minimum*, bush basil – a small-leaved species.

O. b. var. *purpurascens*, purple basil – purple leaves.

                    0.5 × 0.4   Well-drained   Warm sun
....

BAY *LAURUS NOBILIS*
An evergreen shrub or small tree with dark green leathery
leaves and clusters of creamy-yellow flowers in May or June.
The leaves are used dried or fresh in soups, sauces and pickles,

bouquet garni and in meat and fish dishes (especially salmon). Bay trees are often seen clipped into shapes – pyramids or standard balls. Being evergreen, they can provide a structural framework for perennial or annual herbs. There is a gold-leaved variety (*L. nobilis* 'Aurea').

6.0 × 3.0   Fertile, well-drained   Warm sun

BERGAMOT *MONARDA DIDYMA*

An aromatic perennial with attractive red, white, purple or pink flowers arranged in dense terminal clusters from June to August. The leaves are used to make Oswego tea and added to salads. Lemon bergamot (*M. citriodora*) has strongly lemon-scented young leaves used in teas and to flavour game. Wild bergamot (*M. fistulosa*) can be used in the same way.

0.8 × 0.4   Fertile, moist soil   Sun or part shade

BORAGE *BORAGO OFFICINALIS*

An erect annual that seeds itself freely. The leaves and stems are covered in coarse, stiff hairs. The exquisite blue star-shaped flowers that bloom from June to August can be candied and used to decorate cakes. The young leaves have a taste like cucumber and with lemon and honey make a refreshing drink. Bees love the flowers and the resultant honey is of high quality. Since ancient times, borage leaves have been used to flavour and garnish wine cups. More recently the flowers and leaves have become a traditional embellishment to Pimms. There is an interesting white-flowered form.

0.5 × 0.3   Any soil, but prefers well-drained stony soils
Sun or part shade

CAMOMILE *CHAMAEMELUM NOBILE*

Roman or lawn camomile is a low growing, creeping perennial with thread-like leaves. The white daisy flowers appear from May to September. *C. n.* 'Treneague' is the famous non-flowering variety that is supposedly the most suitable for

Bergamot

Borage

Camomile

lawns or camomile seats as it needs very little cutting. But beware, a camomile lawn needs careful preparation and maintenance. It is a labour of love that can easily become a real chore. Roman camomile has an agreeable apple-like scent which made it a popular strewing plant in the Middle Ages. It is a pretty plant for the herb garden but has a bitter taste. German camomile or scented mayweed (*Matricaria recutita*) is the one used for making camomile tea. It is a low growing aromatic annual with feathery foliage and white daisy flowers from May to August. Camomile tea is a soothing drink that aids digestion and acts as a sedative.

0.4 × 0.4   Well-drained, fertile soil   Sun

CHERVIL *ANTHRISCUS CEREFOLIUM*

Chervil is an annual herb with pale green, deeply divided leaves and small, white flowers in May or June. The fresh leaves flavour or decorate salads, soups or sauces. They go especially well with egg dishes. Always add the chopped leaves just before serving. It is popular in France where it helps to

Chervil

Chives

make up *bouquets garnis*. To use fresh all year round, sow a few
seeds successively from early spring to early autumn.

0.4 × 0.3   Well-drained   Partial shade

CHIVES *ALLIUM SCHOENOPRASUM*
A small perennial onion with thin, hollow leaves and beautiful pink pom-pom flower clusters from June to July. Chives
also make an excellent edging plant. The leaves are used raw
chopped into soups, salads, cream cheese or added to eggs,
cooked vegetables or sauces.
A. s. var. *sibiricum* – larger parts and is commonly known as
giant chives.
A. s. 'Forescate' – a more decorative form with large, deep
rose-coloured flowers.

0.2 × 0.2   Any fertile soil   Sun

CLOVE PINK *DIANTHUS CARYOPHYLLUS*
A tufted perennial and one of the earliest cultivated flowers much loved throughout the centuries. Like many cottage garden plants, the clove pink was grown for its decorative, culinary and medicinal properties. The narrow blue-green leaves are topped by highly-scented pink, single or double flowers from July to August. There are a number of named colour selections, many now sadly lost, but you will still find 'Lord Chatham' with salmon-coral flowers, and a few others with red, white, or striped flowers. It was used in vinegars, ales, wines, sauces and salads for its spicy, clove-like aroma. The petals can be dried and used in pot pourris. Although low on usefulness in the kitchen itself, the clove pink combines well with other herbs.

0.3 × 0.3   Well-drained   Sun

COMFREY *SYMPHYTUM OFFICINALE*
A tough large-leaved perennial with drooping clusters of bell-shaped flowers that are blue, purple, pink, cream or white from May to October. Comfrey can be used to make a tea but recent research suggests that it may contain carcinogens. The main reason for its inclusion is that it makes an excellent compost or, fermented in a butt of water, a superb organic

Comfrey

Coriander

liquid fertilizer. It will grow where many plants will not (including damp and dank shade) but can be a little too invasive for the smaller garden. There are many other species and forms of comfrey suitable for the decorative herb garden.

0.8 × 0.8   Any soil, especially moist types   Prefers shade

CORIANDER *CORIANDRUM SATIVUM*
An annual herb with bright green, shiny leaves that are attractively divided. The pale pink flowers appear from June to August. The leaves are used in Egyptian, Peruvian and especially Indian dishes and for flavouring German sausages. Pork cooked with coriander is a traditional Greek dish. It is also used to flavour soups, stews, bread, fruit, sweets, chocolate and many alcoholic drinks especially liqueurs. The seeds are ingredients of curry powder and spice mixtures. Fresh corian-

der can be harvested for many weeks from a whole plant placed in a fridge in a jar of water covered by a plastic bag.

0.4 × 0.3   Well-drained   Sun

DILL *ANETHUM GRAVEOLENS*

A pretty annual herb with feathery blue-green leaves topped by umbels of tiny yellow flowers from June to August that are followed by brown, ribbed seeds. Dill leaves, at their best just before flowering, are used in pickling, in yogurt and many fish dishes, especially those from Scandinavia, such as gravalax. Dill seeds infused in water or wine settle indigestion and induce sleep – hence their use in infant gripe water.

0.8 × 0.6   Moist soil preferred   Sun

ELDER *SAMBUCUS NIGRA*

A deciduous shrub or small tree native to Europe (including Britain) and W. Asia. The creamy-white scented flowers are produced in plate-like bunches from June to July. These are followed by purple-black berries that are ripe by early September. The berries and flowers are used to make jams, jellies, wines (including elder flower champagne) and various beverages as well as in pies, sweets and cakes. Elder flower water is used as a skin lotion and tonic. The leaves can also be used in wines and jams or herbal teas. The straight species is really only attractive when in flower or in fruit. There are many good forms however, with more decorative foliage, for example (see also Checklists):

S. n. 'Aurea' – golden-yellow leaves.
S. n. 'Guincho Purple' –green leaves turning black-purple later.
S. n. 'Laciniata' – cut-leaved variety.

5.0 × 4.0   Any soil   Sun or part shade

FENNEL *FOENICULUM VULGARE*

A tall perennial with stout stems and feathery foliage. The yellow flower umbels appear in July and August. The whole

Dill

Elder

Fennel

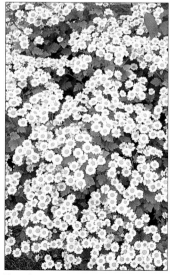

Feverfew

plant smells of aniseed – delicious in a sauce or stuffing. The leaves and stalks are especially good with fish and in marinades for pork or veal, in soups, salads and cakes. The seeds flavour liqueurs or help to scent soaps, perfumes and in water make a soothing eye wash. Fennel is said to aid the digestion of fatty foods and oily fish and is also used to make a tea.

F. v. var. *dulce*, Florence fennel – has a thick basal stalk which can be eaten like celery or boiled or baked as a vegetable.

F. v. 'Purpureum' – bronze fennel with bronze-purple foliage.

1.2 × 0.4   Well-drained loam   Sun

FEVERFEW *TANACETUM PARTHENIUM*

An aromatic perennial with yellowish-green divided leaves and small white daisy flowers with yellow centres from May to October. The only culinary use is cooking the leaves when a degree of bitterness is required. It is also reputed to 'cut' the grease when added to some foods. It is included mainly for its decorative merits. Feverfew is long-flowering with a simple appeal and seeds itself around freely.

T. p. 'Aureum' – a fine yellow-leaved form.

T. p. 'Plenum' – a delightful double-flowered form. There is much interest in feverfew at the moment because of the relief it apparently gives to some migraine sufferers.

0.7 × 0.4   Any soil   Sun

GARLIC *ALLIUM SATIVUM*

A bulbous perennial with linear leaves and pink or whitish flower clusters from June to July. This is a very important culinary herb, considered by many cooks, especially those of Mediterranean origin, to be an essential ingredient in cooking and the basis of many dishes. It is used to flavour soups, stews, vegetables, sauces, oil, mayonnaise, meat and fish. Rub the insides of salad bowls with a cut bulb for a subtle flavour. Garlic is also considered to be an excellent antiseptic and decongestant. Regular consumption is thought to improve general health and reduce high blood pressure. It is easily

Garlic chives   Good King Henry

grown by planting the cloves in spring. *A. tuberosum*, garlic chives, has a mild garlic flavour, delicious when added to salads or cream cheese.

0.4 × 0.4   Well-drained   Sun

GOOD KING HENRY *CHENOPODIUM BONUS-HENRICUS*
A perennial herb with arrow-shaped leaves and yellow-green flowers from May to August. The young leaves have been used for centuries in place of spinach, with a taste that is similar but milder. The young shoots can be boiled and eaten like asparagus. The bruised leaves make a poultice for sore skin.

0.3 × 0.3   Fertile, well-drained   Sun

HORSERADISH *ARMORACIA RUSTICANA*
A perennial with long, fleshy roots and large oval leaves. The white, aromatic flowers appear from June to August. There is a variegated leaved variety. The hot, biting taste of raw horseradish is lost when cooked. The raw root grated or sliced, mixed with cream, white wine vinegar, salt and a little sugar

makes the famous sauce served with beef, ham, smoked trout, mackerel or kippers. The young leaves may be chopped into salads. The root will soothe bites, stings and chilblains.

0.5 × 0.4   Deep, fertile soil   Sun or part shade

....

HYSSOP *HYSSOPUS OFFICINALIS*
A partially evergreen perennial with long spikes of pink, blue or white flowers from June to August. The aromatic flowers and leaves make a delicious addition to salads, game soups, fruit pies and many meat dishes as long as it is used sparingly. It also aids the digestion of greasy meat or fish. Honey made from hyssop flowers is excellent. Hyssop tea helps lung infections, irregular blood pressure and as a lotion for insect stings.
H. o. subsp. *aristatus* – rock hyssop, a compact sort.
Agastache foeniculum – anise hyssop, attractive mauve-purple flowers in late summer. The aniseed-scented leaves are used to make a herbal tea.

0.6 × 0.5   Light, well-drained   Warm sun

....

LAVENDER *LAVANDULA AUGUSTIFOLIA* and
L. × INTERMEDIA
Highly decorative evergreen or semi-evergreen aromatic shrubs, a must for every herb garden or border. The mainly

Horseradish

Hyssop

French Lavender

Lavender Cotton

blue flowers appear above the grey-green foliage throughout summer. Lavender makes a fine centre-piece to a small herb garden or a low edging or hedge. There are many named varieties, including some less effective pink and white forms. The flowers, collected when just in full bloom, are dried for potpourris and sachets. In the kitchen, a small amount of chopped leaves gives an aromatic tang to salads and roast lamb. Lavender water is said to have antiseptic, disinfectant and therapeutic properties. Taken as a mild infusion, lavender is prescribed for headaches, fainting, vertigo and insomnia as it has a sedative and tranquillising effect. For something different, try French lavender (*L. stoechas*) with purple flowers and long lasting bracts or, better still, *L.s.* subsp. *pedunculata* which has very long decorative bracts.

0.3 to 0.6 × 0.4   Any soil except heavy clay or boggy conditions
Sun or a little shade

LAVENDER COTTON *SANTOLINA CHAMAECYPARISSUS*
Compact dwarf shrubs with feathery, aromatic foliage and

yellow or cream flowers in summer. They have no culinary use but their attractive silver, grey or green leaves make them a must for any herb garden – particularly as a low hedge or edging plant. *S. c.* var. *nana* is a dwarf, compact variety.

S. pinnata – a dwarf sub-shrub with very finely divided green leaves.

S. p. subsp. *neapolitana* – lemon-yellow flowers. The varieties 'Edward Bowles' and 'Sulphurea' have grey-green foliage and very pale creamy yellow flowers.

0.8 × 0.8   Poor, sandy soils   Sun

LEMON BALM *MELISSA OFFICINALIS*

A strongly lemon-scented perennial with heart-shaped leaves and white, yellow or pink flowers from June to October. In cooking, use the leaves in fish and poultry dishes, herb sauces, marinades, jams, jellies, puddings and fruit salads. Fresh melissa tea helps induce sleep and is particularly good with peppermint added. It is also used in perfumes, liqueurs and a cordial drink.

M. o. 'Allgold' – gold leaves that scorch unless in shade.

M. o. 'Aurea' – a good gold-variegated form.

0.4 × 0.5   Any soil   Sun or part shade

Lemon Balm

Lemon Verbena

LEMON VERBENA *ALOYSIA TRIPHYLLA*

A tender deciduous shrub ideally suited to pot culture so that it can be brought into a porch or conservatory for the winter months. In summer it will thrive outside on a warm patio or against a south facing wall. The yellow-green leaves are narrow and pointed; the pale lavender flowers appear on slim terminal spikes in July or August. This plant is of no great culinary use nor is it exciting to look at. However, the lemony scent given off from a crushed leaf is incredibly powerful. It is used to make liqueurs, perfumes, potpourris and a refreshing tea.

1.2 × 0.6   Any soil   Warm sun

LOVAGE *LEVISTICUM OFFICINALE*

This is a perennial herb with large, dark green divided leaves that have a strong yeasty odour. The small yellow flowers appear in June and July. The leafstalks can be blanched and eaten like celery and the young leaves added to soups and stews or eaten with new potatoes. The young stems are candied like angelica. Lovage tea stimulates digestion.

1.0 × 0.5   Fertile, moist but well-drained   Sun

MEADOWSWEET *FILIPENDULA ULMARIA*

A native perennial with serrated leaves and fragrant, creamy-white flowers from June to August. In previous centuries meadowsweet was a popular strewing herb; the scent from the flowers filled a room for weeks. Tea made from the dried flowers or roots helps cure urinary problems. Recent research has shown that meadowsweet contains the same chemicals that are used to make aspirin.

F. u. 'Aurea' – completely yellow leaves especially attractive in spring.

F. u. 'Variegata' – splashes of yellow on the leaves.

0.8 × 0.4   Moist soil   Sun or shade

MINT *MENTHA*

The mints are one of the most important groups of culinary herbs. They are used all over the world for both cooking and medicinal purposes. Although very variable in appearance they have similar properties and are interchangeable. Most are invasive and need to be kept under control. Mints are used in sauces and teas; Arabs have drunk mint tea since ancient times. They will also flavour jams, jellies, meat (especially lamb), fish or vegetable dishes. A more modern use for mint is in cocktails, punches, cordials and of course confectionery, soaps and toothpaste. The most popular varieties include:

M. aquatica, watermint – for boggy places, with a powerful scent.

M. pulegium, pennyroyal – with purple flowers, good amongst paving.

M. requienii, Corsican or Spanish mint – tiny leaves with a peppermint smell.

M. spicata 'Crispa', curly mint – with curly bright green leaves.

M. spicata, spearmint – very pungent and very useful.

M. suaveolens 'Variegata', pineapple mint – cream variegated leaves.

M. suaveolens, applemint – large hairy leaves.

M. × gentilis, ginger mint – gold splashed leaves and a slight ginger scent.

M. × piperita, peppermint – reddish tinged young stems and leaves.

M. × p. nm. *citrata*, eau de Cologne mint – a strong lemon scent.

M. × smithiana – red-tinged leaves and stems.

0.1 to 0.7 × 0.2 to 0.8   Fertile, moist soil preferred
Sun or part shade

MYRTLE *MYRTUS COMMUNIS*

An evergreen shrub with aromatic foliage requiring protection in a harsh winter. The creamy white flowers appear from May to August followed by black, fleshy berries which can be used as an alternative to peppercorns. Like many herbs, the use of myrtle for medicinal purposes can be traced back to Greek and Roman times. Along with rosemary it is the evergreen shrub most associated with herb gardens. It is the most appropriate structural or framing plant for herbs. The small, pointed leaves can be used in pot pourris and added to roasting meats at the end of the cooking time. There is a doubleflowered form ('Flore Pleno'), a small-leaved sub-species (*M.o.* subsp. *tarentina*) and variegated forms.

1.5 × 1.0   Well-drained   Warm, sheltered

NASTURTIUM *TROPAEOLUM MAJUS*

A climbing or trailing annual with large red, yellow or orange flowers from May to September. It is often sold as a bedding plant and its vigorous habit can be put to good use on banks and sloping borders. It readily self-seeds and can become a nuisance if not kept under control. The flowers and leaves have a peppery taste and have a high vitamin C content. They

Lovage

Meadowsweet

Spearmint

Pineapple Mint

Nasturtium

Oregano

make a tangy addition to salads. The flowers can also be stuffed. The seeds are added to pickles or used as a substitute for capers. There is a less vigorous speckled leaf form.

3.0 × 3.0   Any soil   Sun or part shade

OREGANO OR WILD MARJORAM *ORIGANUM VULGARE*
This tough European native perennial thrives in poor, dry soils. The aromatic leaves are complemented by rose-lilac flower clusters from June to September. Wild marjoram has a spicy flavour whereas sweet marjoram, *O. majorana*, is sweeter. Pot marjoram, *O. onites*, gives a more acidic flavour and is used to make a tea that improves circulation. Marjoram of whatever type can be used in stuffings with meats or vegetables, especially tomato dishes, in pizzas, spaghetti and to flavour sausages and salamis. It is also used in potpourris and scented sachets.
O. v. 'Compactum' – a low growing variety.
O. v. 'Gold Tip' and 'Aureum Crispum' – yellow-leaved varieties.

0.5 × 0.4   Well-drained, especially chalk   Sun

PARSLEY *PETROSELINUM CRISPUM*
A biennial herb with dark green curly leaves and, in June or July, clusters of yellowish flowers. It has been a popular culinary herb for thousands of years. Rich in vitamins A, B and C, it is an excellent addition to the diet. Use it in making herb mixtures, including *bouquets garnis* or as a garnish to salads, soups, casseroles, new potatoes and fish dishes. Parsley sauce with cold lamb is a popular combination. Some people use parsley as a breath sweetener after eating garlic. Seeds may take a long time to germinate, but, curiously, soaking them in urine overnight will speed the process. French parsley has flat leaves that have a stronger flavour, while Hamburg parsley (*P. c.* var. *tuberosum*) is grown for its edible swollen root, cooked or grated into salads.

0.3 × 0.3   Fertile, cultivated soil, moist   Part shade

ROSEMARY *ROSMARINUS OFFICINALIS*

An aromatic evergreen shrub with blue (or white or pink) flowers in early summer. Introduced into Britain by the Romans it is used to flavour meat, especially lamb, and shell-fish. It can be added to soups, stews and vegetables, often combined with wine or garlic. Rosemary will also flavour jellies, jams, and cakes. It is an excellent plant for attracting bees. The many forms include:

R. o. var. *albiflorus* – white flowers tinged blue.

R. o. 'Benenden Blue' – dark blue flowers excellent for cooking.

R. o. 'Miss Jessopp's Upright' – upright growth.

R. o. 'Fota Blue' – compact.

R. o. 'Frimley Blue' – China blue flowers and spiky foliage.

R. o. 'Majorca Pink' – Lilac-pink flowers.

R. o. 'Roseus' – lilac-pink flowers.

R. o. 'Severn Sea' – excellent free flowering form, spreading habit.

R. o. 'Tuscan Blue' – broader foliage, deep blue flowers.

R. o. Prostratus Group (*R. lavandulaceus* of gardens) – a slightly tender, prostrate with blue flowers.

0.4 to 1.2 × 0.5 to 1.5   Well-drained   Sun

RUE *RUTA GRAVEOLENS*

This evergreen perennial is more attractive than useful. The foliage is fleshy, lobed and misty blue-green in colour. The small green-yellow flower clusters appear from July to August. The strong, pungent leaves were used to deter insects, especially fleas in cottage kitchens. They are used sparingly in salads and alcoholic drinks including grappa. Beware, the leaves and sap can cause a serious skin rash or even blistering.

R. g. 'Variegata' – pretty, cream variegated leaves.

R. g. 'Jackman's Blue' – an improved variety.

0.7 × 0.4   Any soil   Sun

SAGE *SALVIA OFFICINALIS*

The common garden sage is the epitome of a good herb,

Parsley

Rosemary

Rue

Purple-leaved Sage

being both useful and decorative. It is a low-growing, woody plant, virtually evergreen, but responds well to cutting back every spring. The greyish leaves are aromatic and are joined by violet, purple pink or white flower spikes from June to August. Use in stuffings, salads, pickles, cheeses and even kebabs as well as to flavour fish, stews and soups. It makes fatty meat such as pork or duck more digestible. Sage tea is a good general tonic for nerves and circulation. There are many other salvias with culinary uses such as *S. elegans* 'Scarlet Pineapple', the Pineapple Sage which has pineapple-scented leaves used in fruit salads or on roast pork. Others are just stunningly attractive flowering plants, such as *S. patens* (bright blue flowers) and *S. microphylla* var. *neurepia* (crimson flowers) which needs frost protection, but look very much at home in the herb garden.

S. o. 'Albiflora' − is the white-flowers form with narrow leaves.

S. o. 'Icterina' − green and yellow variegated leaves.

S. o. 'Purpurascens' − bronze-red foliage.

S. o. 'Tricolor' – pink and white splashed leaves but is slow to establish and hates winter wet.

0.5 × 1.0   Well-drained soil   Sun

···

SALAD BURNET *SANGUISORBA MINOR*
Salad Burnet is a small tough perennial with distinctive paired leaflets and, in late summer, dark red flower heads. The leaves have been used since medieval times in salads. The nutty, cucumber-like taste is put to good use in soups, stews, cheeses and butters. It also adds a cool flavour to wine cups and cold drinks and is used to make a diuretic tea.

0.4 × 0.4   Well-drained, especially chalk   Sun or shade

···

SORREL *RUMEX ACETOSA*
An erect perennial with broad, arrow-shaped leaves and reddish flower spikes in June and July. The leaves are used in sauces, soups, omelettes and salads and eaten with cold or roast meat – but always use stainless steel knives and non-stick pans as the chemicals in the plant react with iron. Young leaves can be cooked and eaten like spinach. Remove the flowers when they appear to encourage good foliage growth. Sorrel tea is diuretic and the foliage is also used to soothe mouth ulcers, sores and boils. French sorrel (*R. scutatus*) is less

Salad Burnet

Sorrel

Sweet Cicely

Southernwood

likely to flower and has a less bitter taste so is generally more favoured for culinary purposes – especially in sorrel soup and spring salads. *R. sanguineus* var. *sanguineus* is the decorative red-veined dock.

1.0 × 0.5   Any fertile, moist soil   Sun

SOUTHERNWOOD *ARTEMISIA ABROTANUM*
A strongly aromatic shrub with finely divided grey-green leaves and small yellow flowers in August. The leaves have a lemon taste used in cake-making (in France and Italy), salads and vinegars. There are a number of decorative artemisias that are suitable for the herb garden. Some rank amongst the best of all silver-leaved plants (*see also* Tarragon). The bitter-tasting silver leaves of *A. absinthium*, also known as wormwood, are used to make a diuretic tea. Absinthe, the poisonous, addictive liqueur, was made from the roots of wormwood. 'Lambrook Silver' is an improved variety with finer, more silver foliage.

1.0 × 0.8   Sandy soil   Sun

SWEET CICELY *MYRRHIS ODORATA*
An attractive and aromatic perennial with deeply cut, feathery leaves that are light green in colour. The puffs of white blooms appear above the foliage from May to June. The sweetly scented foliage, can be used in cooking tart fruit to reduce the amount of sugar to be added – especially useful for diabetics or slimmers – and the boiled roots can be added to salads. This is a highly decorative plant looking like a cross between a fern and an aristocratic cow-parsley.

0.8 × 0.6   Prefers moist soil   Sun or shade

TANSY *TANACETUM VULGARE*
Tansy is considered a weed by some. It is a native of the waste ground, hedgerows and roadsides of Europe, but the delightful fern-like leaves and heads of yellow button flowers from June to September make it a worthy garden plant. The fresh

Curled Tansy

young leaves can be stewed with rhubarb and used in puddings, cakes and pancakes. Tansy tea made from the flowers and leaves is a good, general tonic. Rubbed over meat, the leaves are said to prevent decay and keep away flies. Curled Tansy (*T. v.* var. *crispum*) has attractive, curly, bright green foliage and can be used in the same ways.

0.8 × 0.4   Any soil   Sun or shade

TARRAGON, FRENCH *ARTEMISIA DRACUNCULUS* var. *SATIVA*

A tender perennial with spreading roots and long, shiny leaves and small yellow flower spikes appearing in late summer. Plants should be protected from winter frost. This is a very important culinary herb, especially in France, with a wide range of uses. It is a vital ingredient in Béarnaise and hollandaise sauces and sauce tartare, and of course tarragon vinegar and butter. It is used to make many classic chicken and fish dishes. Many herb mixtures and stuffings include tarragon. Its popularity in cooking stems from the fact that it has a stimulatory effect on the whole digestive system. Russ-

French Tarragon

ian tarragon (*A. d.* subsp. *dracunculoides*) is very similar but more vigorous and has a much inferior flavour.

0.5 × 0.3   Light soils   Warm, sun

THYME *THYMUS*

A huge group of miniature shrubs with either a creeping or upright habit. There is a wide range of foliage and flower colours and a choice of scents. Thyme is used extensively in the commercial production of cosmetics, perfumes, liquors and soaps. It is also added to potpourris. In cooking, thyme is an essential ingredient in *bouquet garni* and is used to flavour soups, stews, meat and fish dishes as well as vegetables. Taken regularly in food or as a herbal tea, thyme helps maintain good health. Modern research has shown that essence of thyme is strong enough to kill germs in forty seconds. On top of all these wonderful uses, thymes are beautiful plants suitable for containers, amongst rocks or paving, as a border edging or by planting a mixture of thymes together in their own bed you can create a mosaic carpet of colour. The following are some of those readily available (see also Checklists):

T. serpyllum – wild thyme, which has a creeping habit. Forms include:

T. s. coccineus 'Major' – dark crimson flowers.

T. s. albus – white flowers

T. s. 'Annie Hall' – pink flowers, mat forming.

T. s. 'Pink Chintz' – pale pink flowers and grey, hairy leaves.

T. vulgaris – common or garden thyme, has mauve flowers and is the best for cooking. Forms include:

T. v. aureus, golden thyme – pale pink flowers and gold foliage with an orange scent.

T. × citriodorus – lemon thyme has pink flowers and a strong lemon scent. Forms include:

T. × c. 'Archer's Gold' – pink flowers, yellow-flushed foliage.

'Bertram Anderson' – yellow foliage.

'Silver Queen' – silver, variegated foliage.

T. 'Doone Valley' – creeping golden thyme.

T. praecox 'Porlock' – mauve flowers and good dark green foliage.

T. praecox subsp. *arcticus* (syn. *T. drucei*), broad-leaved thyme – deep-pink flowers that last a long time. Very strong flavour.

T. herba-barona – rose-purple flowers and caraway scented leaves.

T. pseudolanuginosus – woolly thyme has grey, hairy leaves.

0.1 to 0.4 × 0.3 to 1.0   Well-drained, especially chalk   Sun

WINTER SAVORY *SATUREJA MONTANA*

An aromatic woody perennial with stiff branches, narrow leaves and pale purple flowers in June. It has a sharp, spicy taste useful for flavouring bean dishes. It can also be used to make stuffings for chicken, in pies, sausages and with eggs or fish dishes. Winter savory aids the digestion of food such as cucumber and pork.

S. hortensis, summer savory – prefers a richer soil and full sun. It has a milder flavour but can be used in much the same way as winter savory.

S. spicigera, creeping savory – a low spreader with white flowers and a strong flavour.

0.3 × 0.3   Light, well-drained   Sun or shade

Thyme

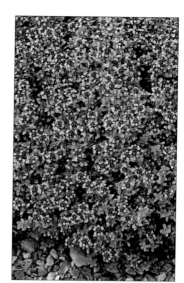

Lemon Thyme

Winter Savory

PLANT CHECKLISTS

....

A FINGERTIP GUIDE TO PLANTS
FOR A HERB GARDEN

THE MOST USEFUL COOKING HERBS

The indispensable culinary herbs that today's cooks and herb gardeners should never be without.

Basil, Sweet *Ocimum basilicum*
Bay *Laurus nobilis*
Chives *Allium schoenoprasum*
Coriander *Coriandrum sativum*
Fennel *Foeniculum vulgare*
Garlic *Allium sativum*
Horseradish *Armoracia rusticana*
Mint *Mentha*
Oregano (Marjoram) *Origanum*
Parsley *Petroselinum crispum*
Rosemary *Rosmarinus officinalis*
Sage *Salvia officinalis*
Tarragon *Artemisia dracunculus*
Thyme *Thymus*

HERBS FOR MAKING TEAS

Anise Hyssop *Agastache foeniculum*
Apothecary's Rose *Rosa gallica*
  var. *officinalis*
Bergamot *Monarda*
Calamint *Calamintha grandiflora*

Camomile, German *Matricaria recutita*
Catnip, Catmint *Nepeta*
Common Flax (Linseed) *Linum usitatissimum*
Common Lime *Tilia × europaea*
Cowslip *Primula veris*
Dandelion *Taraxacum officinale*
Dog Rose *Rosa canina*
Elder *Sambucus nigra*
Fennel *Foeniculum vulgare*
Goldenrod *Solidago*
Herb Robert *Geranium robertianum*
Hop *Humulus lupulus*
Hyssop *Hyssopus officinalis*
Lady's Mantle *Alchemilla mollis*
Lemon Balm *Melissa officinalis*
Lemon Verbena *Aloysia triphylla*
Lovage *Levisticum officinale*
Marsh Mallow *Althaea officinalis*
Mint *Mentha*
Pot Marigold *Calendula officinalis*
Pot Marjoram *Origanum onites*
Rosemary *Rosmarinus officinalis*
Sage *Salvia officinalis*
Salad Burnet *Sanguisorba minor*
Sorrel *Rumex rugosus*
Sweet Violet *Viola odorata*
Sweet Woodruff *Galium odoratum*
Tansy *Tanacetum vulgare*

Thyme *Thymus*
Yarrow *Achillea millefolium*

Caution – some herbs, especially in the form of a tea, have strong effects on the metabolism. Teas can therefore be dangerous if the dosage or recipe is wrong or to people with certain complaints, to pregnant women or children. Always check with experts first or use only under qualified medical supervision.

HERBS ATTRACTIVE TO BEES

Aconite *Aconitum*
Borage *Borago officinalis*
Catmint *Nepeta*
Goldenrod *Solidago*
Hyssop *Hyssopus officinalis*
Lavender *Lavandula*
Lemon Balm *Melissa officinalis*
Mint *Mentha*
Oregano (Marjoram) *Origanum*
Red Valerian *Centranthus ruber*
Rosemary *Rosmarinus officinalis*

Summer Savory *Satureja hortensis*
Thyme *Thymus*
Vipers Bugloss *Echium vulgare*

HERBS FOR POT-POURRIS

Apothecary's Rose *Rosa gallica* var. *officinalis*
Bay *Laurus nobilis*
Bergamot *Monarda*
Borage *Borago officinalis*
Camomile, Roman *Chamaemelum nobile*
Clove Pink *Dianthus caryophyllus* (and other spp).
Hyssop *Hyssopus officinalis*
Lavender Cotton *Santolina*
Lavender *Lavandula*
Lemon Verbena *Aloysia triphylla*
Oregano (Marjoram) *Origanum*
Pot Marigold *Calendula officinalis*
Rosemary *Rosmarinus officinalis*
Scented-leaved Pelargonium *Pelargonium*
Southernwood, etc *Artemisia*
Sweet Woodruff *Galium odoratum*
Thyme *Thymus*

Sage (*Salvia officinalis* 'Tricolor')

HERBS WITH DECORATIVE FOLIAGE

Variegated leaves

Comfrey *Symphytum* 'Hidcote Variegated'
Comfrey *Symphytum* × *uplandicum* 'Variegatum'
Elder *Sambucus nigra* 'Aureomarginata'
Elder *Sambucus nigra* 'Marginata'
Lemon Balm *Melissa officinalis* 'Aurea'
Meadowsweet *Filipendula ulmaria* 'Variegata'
Myrtle *Myrtus communis* 'Variegata'
Myrtle (small-leaved) *Myrtus communis* subsp. *tarentina* 'Microphylla Variegata'
Nasturtium *Tropaeolum majus* 'Variegatum'
Pelargonium *Pelargonium* 'Lady Plymouth'
Pelargonium *Pelargonium crispum* 'Variegatum'
Pineapple Mint *Mentha suaveolens* 'Variegata'
Rue *Ruta graveolens* 'Variegata'
Sage *Salvia officinalis* 'Icterina'
Sage *Salvia officinalis* 'Tricolor'
Thyme *Thymus* × *citriodorus* 'Golden King'
Thyme *Thymus* × *citriodorus* 'Golden Queen'
Thyme *Thymus* × *citriodorus* 'Silver Queen'
Thyme *Thymus* × *citriodorus* 'Variegatus'
(and many others)

Yellow/gold flushed foliage

Bay *Laurus nobilis* 'Aurea'
Elder *Sambucus nigra* 'Aurea'
Elder *Sambucus racemosa* 'Plumosa Aurea'
Elder *Sambucus racemosa* 'Sutherland Gold'
Feverfew *Tanacetum parthenium* 'Aureum'
Ginger Mint *Mentha* × *gentilis*
Hop *Humulus lupulus* 'Aureus'
Lemon Balm *Melissa officinalis* 'Allgold'
Meadowsweet *Filipendula ulmaria* 'Aurea'
Oregano *Origanum vulgare* 'Aureum'
Oregano *Origanum vulgare* 'Aureum Crispum'
Oregano *Origanum vulgare* 'Gold Tip'
Thyme *Thymus* 'Doone Valley'
Thyme *Thymus vulgaris* 'Aureus'
Thyme *Thymus* × *citriodorus* 'Archer's Gold'

Thyme *Thymus × citriodorus*
'Aureus'
Thyme *Thymus × citriodorus*
'Bertram Anderson'

Bronze/Red Foliage

Basil *Ocimum basilicum* var.
  purpurascens
Bronze Fennel *Foeniculum vulgare*
  'Purpureum'
Elder *Sambucus nigra* 'Guincho
  Purple'
Mint *Mentha × smithiana*
Sage *Salvia officinalis*
  'Purpurascens'

Silver/Grey/Bluish Foliage

Alecost *Balsamita major*
Catmint *Nepeta*
Curry Plant *Helichrysum italicum*
Dill *Anethum graveolens*
Lavender *Lavandula*
Lavender Cotton *Santolina*
Mullien *Verbascum*
Pinks *Dianthus*
Rosemary *Rosmarinus*
Rue *Ruta graveolens*
Scented-leaved Pelargonium
  Pelargonium tomentosum (and
  others)
Southernwood *Artemisia*
  abrotanum★
Thyme, French *Thymus vulgaris*
  'French'
Thyme, Woolly *Thymus*
  pseudolanuginosus
Wormwood *Artemisia absinthum*
Yarrow *Achillea*

★Many other artemisias have silver
or grey foliage.

COMMON HERBS THAT PREFER OR TOLERATE EXTREME CONDITIONS

Hot, dry position

Alecost *Balsamita major*
Bay *Laurus nobilis*
Fennel *Foeniculum vulgare*
Garlic *Allium sativum*
Lavender Cotton *Santolina*
Lavender *Lavandula*
Mullien *Verbascum*
Myrtle *Myrtus communis*
Oregano (Marjoram) *Origanum*
Rosemary *Rosmarinus officinalis*
Rue *Ruta graveolens*
Sage *Salvia*
Southernwood, Wormwood and
  others *Artemisia*
Thyme *Thymus*
Winter (and Summer) Savory
  Satureja

Shade or partial shade

Angelica *Angelica archangelica*
Bergamot *Monarda*
Borage *Borage officinalis*
Chervil *Anthriscus cerefolium*
Chives *Allium schoenoprasum*
Comfrey *Symphytum*
Feverfew *Tanacetum parthenium*
Horseradish *Armoracia rusticana*
Lemon Balm *Melissa officinalis*
Meadowsweet *Filipendula ulmaria*
Mint *Mentha*
Nasturtium *Tropaeolum majus*
Parsley *Petroselinum crispum*
Salad Burnet *Sanguisorba minor*
Sorrel *Rumex acetosa*
Sweet Cicely *Myrrhis odorata*
Tansy *Tanacetum vulgare*

Heavy clay soils

Angelica   *Angelica archangelica*
Borage   *Borage officinalis*
Chives   *Allium schoenoprasum*
Comfrey   *Symphytum*
Fennel   *Foeniculum vulgare*
Lemon Balm   *Melissa officinalis*
Lovage   *Levisticum officinale*
Mint   *Mentha*
Nasturtium   *Tropaeolum majus*
Salad Burnet   *Sanguisorba minor*
Sorrel   *Rumex acetosa*
Sweet Cicely   *Myrrhis odorata*

HERBS SUITABLE FOR CONTAINERS

This Checklist includes small, compact plants, those that are invasive and are therefore kept under control in a container and also those that are tender and that in a container can be moved to a protected site in winter.

Basil   *Ocimum basilicum*
Bay   *Laurus nobilis*★
Borage   *Borago officinalis*
Chervil   *Anthriscus cerefolium*
Chives   *Allium schoenoprasum*
Clove pink   *Dianthus caryophyllus*
Feverfew   *Tanacetum parthenium*
Good King Henry   *Chenopodium bonus-henricus*
Hyssop   *Hyssop officinalis* (and others)
Lavender   *Lavandula*
Lavender Cotton   *Santolina*
Lemon Balm   *Melissa officinalis*
Lemon Verbena★
Mint   *Mentha*†
Myrtle   *Myrtus communis*
Nasturtium   *Tropaeolum majus*†
Oregano (Marjoram)   *Origanum*
Parsley   *Petroselinum crispum*
Pot Marigold   *Calendula officinalis*
Rosemary   *Rosmarinus officinalis*
Rue   *Ruta graveolens*
Sage   *Salvia*
Salad Burnet   *Sanguisorba minor*
Tarragon   *Artemisia dracunculus*★
Thyme   *Thymus*
Winter (and Summer) Savory   *Satureja*

★Tender   †Invasive

HERBS FOR GROWING BETWEEN PAVING

Camomile *Chamaemelum nobile*
Corsican or Spanish Mint *Mentha requienii*
Feverfew *Tanacetum parthenium*
Thyme (creeping types) *Thymus* (many)
Winter Savory *Satureja montana*

HERBS FOR GROUND COVER

Comfrey *Symphytum grandiflorum*
Lavender *Lavandula*
Lavender Cotton *Santolina*
Lemon Balm *Melissa officinalis*
Mint *Mentha*
Oregano (Marjoram) *Origanum vulgare*
Rosemary *Rosmarinus* (various)
Sage *Salvia officinalis*
Southernwood, etc *Artemisia* (many)
Thyme *Thymus* (many)

DECORATIVE CULINARY HERBS FOR THE MIXED BORDER

Angelica *Angelica archangelica*
Bergamot *Monarda*
Borage *Borago officinalis*
Chives *Allium schoenoprasum*
Pinks *Dianthus*
Fennel *Foeniculum vulgare*
Feverfew *Tanacetum parthenium* (varieties of)
Hyssop *Hyssopus officinalis*
Lavender *Lavandula*
Lavender Cotton *Santolina*
Meadowsweet *Filipendula ulmaria*
Mint *Mentha*
Oregano (Marjoram) *Origanum vulgare* (varieties of)
Rue *Ruta graveolens*
Sage *Salvia officinalis* (and others)
Southernwood etc. *Artemisia*
Sweet Cicely *Myrrhus odorata*
Tansy, Curled *Tanacetum vulgare* var. *crispum*
Thyme *Thymus*

PLANTS THAT COMPLEMENT HERBS

This is a general list of plants that are suitable for inclusion in a herb garden or are traditionally associated with herbs. It includes both decorative and structural or framing plants and some decorative/medicinal herbs and vegetables not included in the Directory.

Bears Breeches *Acanthus*
Box *Buxus sempervirens*
Bugle *Ajuga reptans*
Calamint *Calamintha*
Catmint *Nepeta*
Chaste Tree *Vitex agnus-castus*
Chicory *Cichorum intybus*
Christmas Rose *Helleborus niger*
Clary Sage *Salvia sclarea*
Cowslip *Primula veris*
Curry Plant *Helichrysum italicum*
Evening Primrose *Oenothera*
Foxglove *Digitalis*
Heartsease *Viola tricolor*
Heliotrope *Heliotropium peruvianum*
Hollyhock *Alcea rosea*
Honeysuckle *Lonicera periclymenum*
Hop *Humulus lupulus*

Jacob's Ladder *Polemonium caeruleum*
Jerusalem Sage and others *Phlomis*
Joe Pye Weed *Eupatorium purpureum*
Lady's Mantle *Alchemilla mollis*
Lily of the Valley *Convallaria majalis*
Lungwort *Pulmonaria*
Mallow *Malva*
Medlar Tree *Mespilus germanica*
Mexican Orange Blossom *Choisya ternata*
Mulberry *Morus*
Opium Poppy *Papaver somniferum*
Oxslip *Primula elatior*
Primrose *Primula vulgaris*
Purple Orach *Atriplex hortensis* 'Rubra'
Red Valerian *Centranthus ruber*
Roses (Old-fashioned, Species & Shrub Roses) *Rosa*
Soapwort *Saponaria officinalis*
Sweet Violet *Viola odorata*
Thrift *Armeria maritima*
Walnut Tree *Juglans regia*
Yarrow *Achillea*

Note – There are many other plants, particularly perennials such as campanula, geranium, peony, phlox, etc that are associated with cottage gardens that look well with herbs.

The Herb Society, PO Box 415, London SW1P 2HE

Herb suppliers

Most garden centres, plant centres and nurseries offer a wide range of herbs – particularly in the spring. Specialist growers and suppliers include:

Arne Herbs, Limeburn Nurseries, Limeburn Hill, Chew Magna, Avon BS18 8QW

Elsworth Herbs, Avenue Farm Cottage, 31 Smith Street, Elsworth, Cambridgeshire CB3 8HY

Daphne ffiske Herbs, Rosemary Cottage, Bramerton, Norwich, Norfolk NR14 7DW

Herb & Heather Centre, West Haddlesey, nr. Selby, North Yorkshire Y08 8QA

The Herb Garden, Plant Hunter's Nursery, Capel Ulo, Pentre Berw, Gaerwen, Anglesey, Gwynedd LL60 6LF

Hollington Nurseries, Woolton Hall, Newbury, Berkshire RG15 9XT

Iden Croft Herbs, Frittenden Rd, Staplehurst, Kent TN12 0DH

Oak Cottage Herb Garden, Nesscliffe, nr. Shrewsbury, Shropshire, SY4 1DB

Scotland Farmhouse Herbs, Virginstow, Beaworthy, North Devon EX21 5EA

Sellett Hall Herbs, Whittington, via Carnforth, Lancashire LA6 2QF

Poyntzfield Herb Nursery, nr. Balbair, Black Isle, Dingwall, Highland IV7 8LX

Wye Valley Herbs, The Nurtons, Tintern, Chepstow, Gwent NP6 7NX

Herb gardens open to the public
(Check opening times before visiting)

Acorn Bank, Penrith, Cumbria

Chelsea Physic Garden, Chelsea, London

Hardwick Hall, Chesterfield, Derbyshire

Hatfield House, Hatfield, Hertfordshire

Hollington Nursery, Woolton Hall, Berkshire

The Queen's Garden, Kew Palace, Royal Botanic Gardens, Kew, Richmond, Surrey

Leeds Castle, Maidstone, Kent

The Herb Garden at Sissinghurst Castle, Sissinghurst, Kent

Westbury Court, Westbury-on-Severn, Gloucestershire

The Herb Garden at Royal Horticultural Society's Garden, Wisley, Surrey

PICTURE ACKNOWLEDGEMENTS

b–bottom/c–centre/l–left/r–right/t–top
Heather Angel 43 (tr)
British Library/Bridgeman Art Library 7
Eric Crichton front cover inset, 11, 12, 27 (tl & b), 28, 30,
33 (tl, tr & br), 35 (r), 38, 39, 43 (tl & bl), 47 (tl, tr & b),
50 (tl, tr & b), 52, 53, 55 (tl & b), 57, 61
Giraudon/Bridgeman Art Library 6
Jerry Harpur front cover background (Elizabeth Banks, Telegraph
Garden), 62 (designer Simon Hopkinson)
Andrew Lawson 18, 21, 23, 24, 25 (l & r), 27 (tr), 29, 31, 35 (l),
37 (l & r), 44 (b)
Mansell Collection 9
S. & O. Mathews 33 (bl), 36, 44 (t), 55 (tr)
Clive Nichols back cover, 1, 5, 48, 60
John Noot Galleries, Broadway, Worcestershire / Bridgeman
Art Library 16
Photos Horticultural 40, 49
Harry Smith Collection 43 (br), 58